EAGLES

Rourke Enterprises, Inc.
Vero Beach, Florida 32964

PHOTO CREDITS

© Jeff Foott/DRK Photo: Page 7;
© Chuck J. Lamphiear/DRK Photo: Page 17;
© Stephen J. Krasemann/DRK Photo: Page 21;
© Lynn M. Stone: all other photos.

ACKNOWLEDGMENTS

The author wishes to thank the following for
photographic assistance in the preparation of this
book: Chicago Zoological Society (Brookfield Zoo);
Florida Audubon Society; Florida's Weeki Wachee

Library of Congress Cataloging-in-Publication Data

Stone, Lynn M.
  Eagles.

  (The Bird discovery library)
  Includes index.
  Summary: An introduction to the largest bird of prey, one which
can be found worldwide and is the national symbol of the United
States.
  1. Eagles—Juvenile literature. [1. Eagles] I. Title.
II. Series: Stone, Lynn M. Bird discovery library.
QL696.F32S86 1989   598'.916   88-26427
ISBN 0-86592-321-3

TABLE OF CONTENTS

EAGLES

Eagles are among the largest and most powerful **birds of prey.** They are related to hawks, vultures, buzzards, kites, and falcons. Like their relatives, eagles have hooked beaks and sharp toe claws called **talons.** They use their talons to kill other animals for food. These animals are their **prey.**

Nearly 60 different kinds of hunting birds are known as eagles. Many of them have feathers growing all the way to their toes. Scientists call these the "true" eagles.

The bald eagle *(Haliaeetus leucocephalus)* and golden eagle *(Aquila chrysaetos)* are the only eagles normally found in North America.

WHERE THEY LIVE

Eagles live on all continents except Antarctica. Some kinds, or **species,** of eagles live in wet jungles. Others prefer grassland, forest, seacoast, or mountains.

The bald eagle, the national symbol of the United States, lives along rivers, lakes, or the seashore.
The golden eagle lives in the mountains of the western United States, Mexico, and Canada. Few golden eagles live in the eastern United States.

Bald Eagle Feeding on Fish

HOW THEY LOOK

Eagles seem to wear a scowl. They aren't really angry. Some eagles are not even fierce, but birds can not change their expressions.

The color of an eagle's **plumage,** its feathers, depends on the species of eagle. Most eagles are brown or black, often with white trim.

The largest eagles weigh nearly 30 pounds. Females are larger then males.

The average golden eagle is about 35 inches long and weighs 12 pounds. Bald eagles are about the same size.

Eagles have long, broad wings. The wings stretch eight feet across in the largest species.

Tawny Eagle
(Aquila rapax) of Africa

THE EAGLE'S WEAPONS

An eagle's talons are strong and sharp. The eagle often lives on what it kills, and its talons are its weapons.

Many eagles, including the bald and golden, sight their prey from high in the sky. They dive and, with talons outstretched, strike their prey like a hammer.

An eagle's beak is strong and sharp, too. An eagle uses its beak to cut, trim, and tear the prey while its talons grasp it.

Talons and Feet of Bald Eagle

Bald Eagle

THE EAGLE'S DAY

No one knows how each kind of eagle spends its days. Many eagles travel over huge areas and live in very hard-to-reach places. It is often hard to study wild eagles.

Scientists have studied bald eagles, however. Bald eagles usually hunt soon after dawn if they are hungry. If not, they perch on a branch and carefully clean their feathers. The bald eagle calls *kik-kik-kik* if it is disturbed.

Later in the day, the eagle may fly. Sometimes he will hunt, and other times he will soar on currents of air called **thermals.**

Before nightfall, the eagle returns to his roost. This is a tree branch or cliff where the eagle will spend the night. Unlike owls, eagles are active only during the day.

Bald Eagle with Fish

EAGLE NESTS

Many eagles build huge, bulky nests in trees or on cliffs. The tawny eagle *(Aquila rapax)* sometimes nests on the ground.

Bald, golden, and other large eagle species mate for life. Each year the pair returns to the same nest and adds more nesting material, mostly sticks. An old eagle nest, built over a period of many years, may weigh several hundred pounds.

Doris Mager, known in Florida as the "Eagle Lady," once spent several days sitting in a huge bald eagle nest. The attention she received helped to create concern for America's eagles.

Golden Eagle Baby in Nest

BABY EAGLES

Some kinds of eagles lay just one egg. Others lay two or three. The female eagle does most of the incubating, or sitting on the eggs to keep them warm. The eggs hatch six or seven weeks after they have been laid. Meanwhile, the male eagle brings food to the female.

Baby eagles, called eaglets, are helpless. They depend on their parents for food and shade from the sun. In many eagle nests, the older chick kills its younger nestmate.

An eagle grows quickly. After 10 or 11 weeks in the nest, it begins flying.

A wild eagle may live 20 years or longer. Eagles in zoos often reach age 40.

Bald Eagle, Young Adult

PREY

Large eagles are the most powerful bird **predators** on earth. Predators are animals that hunt and kill other animals for food.

Eagles have very keen eyesight to find prey and amazing strength to kill it. Eagles can kill animals three or four times their weight, although they rarely do. Eagles also feed on animals that are already dead.

Most eagles eat a variety of animals. The bald eagle, for example, eats ducks, coots, fish, and many other animals. The Bataleur eagle *(Terathopius ecaudatus)* of Africa has a more specialized diet. The Bataleur is one of the snake-eating eagles.

African Fish Eagle
(Haliaeetus vocifer)

EAGLES AND PEOPLE

The eagle's size, strength, and beauty have made it a popular bird. But its size and strength have also brought it problems. People have shot eagles just because they are big targets. Ranchers have destroyed eagles because they believed that eagles killed their sheep and calves. In fact, eagles rarely kill farm animals.

The eagles' biggest problem though is finding a place to live. The **habitat,** or living space, of eagles is becoming smaller as people cut down forests and build new towns.

By saving the eagle's habitat, we can help save these great birds of prey.

GLOSSARY

Birds of Prey (Birds uhv PRAY)—birds which feed on other animals and have hooked beaks and talons.

Habitat (HAB i tat)—an animal's home surroundings

Incubate (INK you bate)—to keep eggs warm until they hatch

Plumage (PLOO maj)—the covering of feathers on a bird

Predator (PRED a tor)—an animal that kills another animal for food

Prey (PRAY)—an animal which is hunted for food by another animal

Roost (ROOST)—the place where a bird goes to rest, such as a branch

Species (SPEE sheez)—within a group of closely related animals, such as eagles, one certain kind

Talons (TAL ons)—long, hooked claws on the feet of birds of prey

Thermal (THUR mull)—a rising current of air, helpful to soaring birds

INDEX